Shinemaster

Also by Michael Mcfee

Poetry
Earthly
Colander
To See (with photographer Elizabeth Matheson)
Sad Girl Sitting on a Running Board
Vanishing Acts
Plain Air

Anthologies
This Is Where We Live: Short Stories
    by 25 Contemporary North Carolina Writers
The Language They Speak Is Things to Eat: Poems
    by Fifteen Contemporary North Carolina Poets

Shinemaster

poems by
Michael McFee

Carnegie Mellon University Press
Pittsburgh 2006

Acknowledgments

Thanks to these magazines, their editors and readers, for first publishing the following poems:

Agni Review: "Over"
Georgia Review: "Visible Boy"
Grantmakers in the Arts Reader: "Sneezing"
Hogtown Creek Review: "The Culvert," "The Tape," "The Tree Man"
Hudson Review: "Time Enough," "The Wedding Band," "Curtains"
Independent Weekly: "Plenty," "Surely"
Iron Mountain Review: "Vineswinging," "Meteor Shower,"
    "'Helen, Come Forth!'"
Mantis: "Cafeterias"
Nantahala Review: "The Nudists," "Old Pillow"
News & Observer: "Partners," "Rosin Bag"
Oxford American: "Solo," "Spitting"
Paris Review: "Spigot with Imaginary Animals"
Poetry: "Valentine's Afternoon," "Icewater in a Tumbler"
Sandhills Review: "Belching"
Southern Cultures: "The Lessons"
Southern Review: "Spitwads," "Riffs," "Rings of Fire,"
    "'Service Is Our Business,'" "Whistling"
Tar River Poetry: "The Tub," "Roof Ball"
Tri-Quarterly: "Kissing"
Two Rivers Review: "Skin"
Virginia Quarterly Review: "Shinemaster"

Thanks also to Emory & Henry College for printing "Surely" as a broadside on the occasion of their 21st annual literary festival. And many thanks to Brian Carpenter and Alan Shapiro, for helpful advice and encouragement.

Book and cover designed by Michael Szczerban

The publication of this book is supported by a grant from the Pennsylvania Council on the Arts.

PENNSYLVANIA
COUNCIL
ON THE
ARTS

Library of Congress Control Number: 2005924488
ISBN- 13: 978-0-88748-446-9
ISBN- 10: 0-88748-446-8

10 9 8 7 6 5 4 3 2 1

Contents

for Michael Chitwood

Plenty

The battered pickup's bed
is a cornucopia
overflowing with sweet potatoes,
long tapered tubers
irregular and glorious as clouds
backlit by an orange sunset,
headed for roadside stand or market
or maybe back to Europe
where Spanish explorers, just home
from the New World, introduced them
half a millennium ago
as *batatas*, possessed (they insisted)
of aphrodisiacal powers,
which later inspired son-hungry Henry VIII
to import huge quantities
and gorge himself on sweet potatoes
baked into pie after pie
the way my father's mother cooked them,
with light brown sugar
and cinnamon and nutmeg and cloves,
those spices teasing the warmth
out of the smooth meat
that had banked its glowing coal
underground all summer long,
waiting to feed the family
and every famished ancestor
with elemental sweetness,
filling our mouths
with temporary plenty
bite after bite.

Riffs

The mockingbird on the chimneytop
lavishly quotes the world's lavish notes
for the sheer loud fun of it, relishing

how roundly all his mimicky triplets
keep echoing down the empty column
of which he is the ornate capital,

his voice megaphoned into the fireplace
now blazing with the dazzling phrases
of every mortal noise within earshot,

improvising and improving on
the meager graceless notes of rival birds
and pets in heat and clamorous humans,

their horns and telephones and rusty hinges
part of this uncut documentary
that sings things as they eloquently are,

the music of the jazzy hemispheres
filling my head in this little April room
until I'm almost deaf with such sharp riffs:

O good gray bird, Whitman's loquacious ghost,
your solitary throat still shuttling
between oblivion and paradise,

come sit on my tombstone some early spring,
sing till that solid granite comes alive,
make it a fluent flue, an airy shaft

that reaches the rest of the still way down
to where I lie waiting to hear you convert
the spacious green heaven I left above

into a fresh deck of sounds you deal again,
remembering the time I stood transfixed
by your singing poured into that living room,

holding my aching throat as your music—
that chimney's sweetest smoke, returning home—
drove everything but music from the air.

Solo

Apollo, St. Cecilia, what was I doing
the summer I decided to build a guitar from scratch?
I couldn't buy one on my allowance
and knew my parents wouldn't be able to afford
even the cheapest pawnshop model,
so I worked with leftovers we had around the house:
odd plywood scraps, wire nails in jars,
and rubber bands my mom had saved in envelopes.

I had no idea how to work with tools
but went to the basement when nobody was home
to saw and hammer and glue and sand
until it was finished, a trapezoidal box so bizarre
it looked either primitive or futuristic,
an instrument no human in this century or millennium
could possibly have meant to create,
a warping piecemeal thing, the flimsiest lyre ever.

Melodious ones, for the longest time
I couldn't see how ludicrous it was, the fingerboard
with drawn-on frets and position marks,
the head with staggered nails instead of tuning keys,
the jagged sound hole that gave back
every sour plunk I could manage while lip-synching
into the mirror I'd hidden down there,
pretending I was John in the Cavern, *yeah yeah yeah*,

all the manic girls screaming so loud
they couldn't hear me fingering that splintery guitar,
that homemade Fender I strapped on
with a wide belt my dad once used to threaten me:
alone I made it, alone I played it
until one day when suddenly everything seemed stupid,
my solo act in the dank half-dark,
this crude thing in and of my hands, so I snapped it

over my knee with surprising ease
and that dissonance made a strangely pleasing music
as did the fire I built at the back
of the backyard, poking it so no evidence would be left
of my folly but charred wood and ashes
and smoke whose song will sting the blinking eyes
of any honest god or man or boy
who knows what it's like to be immortal for a while.

Spitwads

Little paper cuds we made
by ripping the corners or edges
from homework and class notes
then ruminating them into balls
we'd flick from our fingertips
or catapult with pencils
or (sometimes after lunch)
launch through striped straws
like deadly projectiles
toward the necks of enemies
and any other target where they'd
stick with the tiniest splat,
I hope you're still there,
stuck to unreachable ceilings
like the beginnings of nests
by generations of wasps
too ignorant to finish them
or under desktops with blunt
stalactites of chewing gum,
little white words we learned
to shape and hold in our mouths
while waiting to let them fly,
our most tenacious utterance.

Belching

Behold, they belch out with their mouth. —Psalm 52:7

Not *burp*, that mild onomatopoetic verb

one does into a handkerchief at high tea,
nor *eructation*, pedantic clinical term,

but *belch*, rowdy Anglo-Saxon cousin

to yell, bellow, bawl, howl, and retch,
anarchic fraternal twin to furtive *fart*

though less repressed, more fun-loving,

raw sound on the vernacular verge of speech
if you had a coach like little Jeff Nichols,

who wore taps on his loafers to sound big

and taught us junior-high smart-alecks
the art of belching, how to gulp and vomit

the right amount of air then shape our barks

into resonant names and oaths and jokes,
the daily *I pledge a lesion to the flag*

or *There once was a girl from Nantucket*

or *I am the walrus goo goo g'joob*, anything
to amuse our brothers in the vulgar tongue

and disgust the proper ladies young and old:

it was the flip side of Chipmunks' falsetto,
it was the virile voice we didn't yet have,

it was the gift of gas, our startling breath

resurrected in echoing lockers and stalls
and down the halls and in the backs of buses

again and again until our guts were aching

with giving up the spirit, with gastrolalia,
Fourscore and seven beers ago, eat me, a-men.

The Culvert

The other boys could pelt your ass with crabapples
or sic mutts on your face once you neared the far end
but once you'd crawled a few yards into the dim pipe
tunneling under the road whose cracked pavement
led from your dirt driveways to the modern world
you were all alone and wishing you hadn't accepted
the double-dog-dare to better some numskull's time
by scrabbling escapee-like through that putrid tube
whose diameter was barely greater than your body
clawing over debris that had piled up in the middle
the same way clumsy fate would soon trap you
if the heavy overhead earth didn't crush you first
or a cloudburst drown everything stuck in that gut
before you could worm back toward remembered air
where your fingers might hook a rough concrete lip
and haul your filthy self back into reborn morning
as the cries of the boys echoed back down the culvert.

Visible Boy

The girls in freshman P.E. barely noticed
when I came in to set up their sex-ed movie
"Our Changing Bodies" on the old Bell & Howell,

clanking the twelve-inch reel out of its canister,
clicking it onto the raised arm, threading the film
through an intricate maze of gates and sprockets

until I could finally tuck it into the take-up reel
and turn the projector on, its bum gears jerking
and fluttering as I tried to calm them down,

focusing, framing, then lifting the flickering
window of fingered light onto the opposite wall:
when the movie started counting backwards

I had to leave the classroom and wait outside,
listening to the muffled voice-over and giggles,
the gasps and yucks and disbelieving silence

until something went wrong or the movie was over
and coach knocked on the door to summon me back
to a roomful of girls blinking in strange brightness,

watching me in a new way as I quickly started
to splice or tinker or rewind, avoiding their eyes
looking not so much at as through or inside me,

seeing what they now had scientific terms for,
studying what waited deep in the male of the species,
eager to unspool, to spill, to spoil everything.

Vineswinging

We were aching to achieve escape velocity
in the moonstruck summer of '69
so we'd roam the mountain like renegade Scouts
with rusty hatchets and machetes,
looking for vines hanging from the tallest trees,
bellropes perfect for ringing the sky—
not a thick hairy cable or skinny clothesline
but one that filled the hands like a favorite bat.
We'd test them by tugging, then yanking,
then hanging on (all three of us)
like too much bait: when a vine finally held
we hacked it loose from the forest floor
high enough that one of us could pull it upslope
to get a headlong running start
before leaping into nothing, sweeping out
and up as far as that pendulum would carry him
over the world receding below
before tarzanning back through the trees
to land on legs that had just walked across air.
My mother warned us, said we needed
somewhere safe to splash down
like when she and her friends would drop from vines
into the holy waters of Lake Junaluska,
but we just laughed and kept taking turns
launching ourselves, lording it over the mountain
and the homebodies in the lowly valley,
vineswinging until our hands could no longer grip
and we sprawled dizzy from all the to and fro,
the planet spinning drunkenly under us.
Finally, late one afternoon, summer almost done,
at the absolute outmost point of my arc
over the steepest drop we'd found,
an astronaut at apogee, the earth forgotten,
one giant swing for mankind,
something went very wrong in the canopy

far above and behind me: the vine had pulled free,
my lifeline gone slack, momentum
shifting not backward as usual but farther out
and down in a sudden rush,
in a freefall I knew would break my soaring bones
though I continued clinging to that umbilical cord
as if it could somehow save me
from the gravity ready to rein us boys in.

Mrs. Rembrandt

We called her Mrs. Rembrandt, the artsy lady
who lived in the big ugly house at the corner
but spent most days in her front yard's studio
drawing and doing paintings on a tall easel
far from her kids with their homely dirty faces
and her loud beergut husband the contractor
who'd improvised their home from surplus bricks.

She'd made him gouge a shallow pond from the clay
and build an arching footbridge over one end
so she could order some imported water lilies
and sit on a bench, in a tilted French beret,
painting the exotic scene again and again.
We didn't know enough to call her Mrs. Monet
but ignorance didn't keep us from laughing

when the afternoon bus let out and there she was,
oblivious to the squealing brakes and scholars,
her smock filthier with color than her canvas,
or when she held a weekend Sidewalk Art Show
to which only the mothers went, returning home
with flyers announcing a Summer Sketching Camp
for neighborhood children, at reasonable rates.

It was too late; they'd already signed us up.
And so, for several embarrassed weeks that July,
we groaned down the hill to Mrs. Rembrandt's house
to "improve ourselves" for three eternal hours.
The lucky thing was, the lessons were inside,
where no passersby could see us being artistic
in that vast unfurnished concrete basement

with its damaged doors and windows jammed open
to capture the watery light from the lily pond
she never mentioned or took us out to sketch.

Was she afraid we might spoil the place somehow,
steal its essence with our primitive drawings?
Or was she saving that refuge for herself,
for the rest of the bright solitary day and year?

We wielded fresh pencils, charcoals, and pastels,
struggling with shadowing, perspective, still life
until we finally got to her favorite, portraits,
"the human face divine," as she kept calling it,
first our own self-conscious likeness in a mirror,
then her children, who were just too dull as subjects,
then herself, though she couldn't keep her eyes still

or stop leaning forward to see if we'd discovered
the textbook geometry underlying her face.
At last she paired us up, one boy and one girl
staring at each other across a sawhorse table.
We'd never studied the opposite sex that long
or that hard, face to naked unaverted face,
but we looked closely enough that we all knew

our pencils tentatively scritching across paper
weren't close to capturing what we really saw—
which is where Mrs. Rembrandt suddenly stepped in,
her right hand covering ours and briskly moving
in clear strong strokes across the astonished page
until every portrait looked more or less the same:
big eyes, long lashes, perfectly symmetrical faces

that were like us only better, an idealized version
of our features that gave us kids the utter creeps
but might delight our culture-hungry mothers
as it delighted our teacher, gazing kindly down
at the human faces she'd made more nearly divine,
then up at us, then out at the waiting water
whose beauty she made more beautiful every day.

The Nudists

I found their snapshot buried at the bottom
of my parents' jumbled bedside table drawer:
a normal couple, somewhere out-of-doors,
smiling big for the camera, holding hands,
each of them wearing black socks, blacker shoes,
and nothing else: naked, totally naked
and totally unaroused or unashamed,
just standing there like it was no big deal.

And then my mother walked in. I was caught
not with one of the girlie magazines
(a teasing peek at breasts, some skin, no more)
borrowed from older boys across the street
but with this photo she and dad had hidden,
this dangling Adam, this pale and drooping Eve.
Their pubic hair was deeper than outer space.

"Who are these people?" My voice nearly broke.
"Oh, those are just the nudists, dear," she said,
then took the picture and waited till I left
and firmly closed the bedroom door behind me.

I never found that friendly pair again,
though later I learned there were some naturists
who ran a colony in the next county,
way out in the hills, a place called Eden View.
Did my parents ever go, or think about it,
before two children ruined both their bodies?
And did they meet the nudists in the snapshot,
emigrants from the Empire of the Clothed
to a place where only sun and wind dressed them?
Or did they just like to look at him and her
before or after love, or now and then,
a smaller younger happier version
of what they were, of what they might have been?

Skin

is a casing the spirit would like to shed,
a crust, a mortal film.

The elements hate skin too,
burning or blowing or soaking or rotting

until it can be picked off in little strips,
bodies flaying themselves.

Sometimes it does disappear—
underwater, during music, together in bed

in the slip of original skin across skin,
into skin, yielding skin—

but it comes back harder
and colder than before, the skeleton's ice

freezing the skin until it's finally blue,
the color of birth or death,

the color of otherworldly hope
no human can bear to touch for very long.

Kissing

The mouth's elegy to itself. —Adam Phillips

"It's a pity I can't kiss myself," Freud says

we're saying when we seek out another mouth
as children and later as sublimated adults

in this "softened hint of the sexual act,"

and maybe he's right, but it really does seem
that there's nothing *less* selfish than kissing:

even the most routine hello or goodbye buss

is a surrender of self, a willing sacrifice
of voice and sight and a moment's control,

to say nothing of lovers resuscitating each other

so long their slick lips ache from sharing breath
and teasing it out to one slow crescendo

of lick and suck and smack and salty bite

after another, the kisser and kissee
disappearing into a single body

as Rodin showed us in unbroken stone,

the man's huge hand on the woman's thigh
and her left arm pulling his head down to hers

part of the same mass as the roughhewn rock

they rise from like Adam and Eve discovering
how sour and sweet a mortal kiss can be,

farewell and welcome, betrayal and betrothal,

the smothering of speech and yet a kind
of articulation, a wordless word, unutterable

except by two human beings who agree

to stop and join their mouths in such a manner
that they begin saying the x that is a kiss.

Valentine's Afternoon

Four lanes over, a plump helium heart—

slipped, maybe, from some kid's wrist
or a rushed lover's empty passenger seat

through a half-cracked car window—

rises like a shiny purple cloudlet
toward today's gray mess of clouds,

trailing its gold ribbon like lightning

that will never strike anything
or anyone here on the forsaken ground,

its bold LOVE increasingly illegible

as it ascends over the frozen oaks,
riding swift currents toward the horizon,

a swollen word wobbling out of sight.

Time Enough

"We have to stop," she said when kissed.
"We really have to stop," she said when kissed,
lifting her always-ticking wrist.

"We must be quick," she said at one.
"Listen, we must be quick," she said at one,
her bare skin savored by the sun.

At two she said nothing at all.
At two she said nothing, nothing at all,
asleep in a delicious sprawl.

"I've got to leave," she said at three.
"I've got to leave *right now*," she said at three,
then slowly lifted up one knee.

"I must be home," she said, "by four.
I must be home *or else*," she said, "by four."
Her clothes kept waiting on the floor.

"I don't have time for an affair.
I simply don't have time for this affair,"
she said, refastening her hair,

she said, unfastening her hair,
she said, again refastening her hair
in the dim mirror's lazy glare.

Rings of Fire

The weepy slipnotes of "Last Date,"
the lovesick *burns-burns-burns* of "Ring of Fire"—

the soundtrack to forlorn sunny afternoons
that summer almost forty years ago
when Sally Dixon, who packed meat at Armour all week,
would pack herself into a skirted two-piece
and lie on a warped chaise lounge in her front yard
and guzzle the champagne of bottled beers
till she fell asleep or passed out, hard to tell which,

while Floyd Cramer or Johnny Cash
performed the same encore again and again and again

because she'd put her record player in the window
with the tone arm back so it would repeat
and she could drink and cry and burn her pasty skin
and forget whoever it was she didn't have anymore
until her neighbors shouted out their windows
or tried to call her, though nobody answered
no matter how long they let the phone ring and ring

as Floyd kept slurring those sad wordless tones
or Johnny kept falling *down, down, down*

and Sally kept lying there soaking them up
even after the sun's blunt needle
reached the end of the song it would repeat tomorrow:
what a good bad example she was supposed to be
to us kids who would later stage our own solo shows
featuring too much beer and burning love
and music whose hurt helped, who would never forget

every doomed second of "Last Date" and "Ring of Fire,"
even the backup singers warning *ooh* and *ah*.

Over

One morning, after it was all over,
he looked to his right out the tall window
and saw not the usual oak
but a ghostly film interposing itself
between himself and the world he once knew,

a negative of the night he'd pressed her
against this pane, merely kissing at first,
her back sweating a thin fog
through her t-shirt against the cooling glass,
her body's living breath lingering there,

then bare skin smearing a slow upward swirl
as they lifted each other in dim silence,
a new moon their only light,
his fingerprints dotting the windowpane
as he pushed his moist hands over and past

her sunken shoulders, collecting himself,
leaving these greasy clouds of evidence
he now tried to wipe away
as if they'd never gathered in this room,
as if such touch could ever be erased.

The Wedding Band

It had been slipped on so easily
so long ago,
but now he just couldn't pull it off:
the ring had shrunk
below his long-married thick knuckle
and it was stuck,
stranded around its namesake finger,
a dull halo
choke-collaring his soon-to-be-single digit

until he tried
cooking oil and profane wrenching,
his free right hand
eventually freeing his lassoed left one,
the wedding band
bowling its gold *oh* across the kitchen floor
as he studied
the greasy, raw-looking, strangely naked skin
where it had been,

the base of that finger atrophied,
a broken limb
just out of its cast, pale and withered,
still circumscribed
by the thin dent that bond had imprinted,
a ghostly ring
whose phantom pressure would never quite
unmarry him
no matter how hard he rubbed the girdled flesh.

The Tape

The unspooled videotape in the roadside ditch
glistens as cars pass, a dark rivulet.
I stop at the broken case, labeled OUR WEDDING—
no date, no place, no names, a private record
somebody no longer wanted, a tiresome pet
they'd driven way out into the countryside
to dump off, but then destroyed so nobody else
could see or hear that long-planned whitest day.
How many times did anybody watch this tape?
It stretches straight out of sight over the rise,
as if its flat unmarked length could somehow measure
the distance from *I do* to mute divorce
to that blank moment when ex-bride or -groom
laid down this black wedding ribbon then drove away.

Sneezing

Damn braces. Bless relaxes. —Blake

It's always surprising when somebody sneezes

and an utter stranger quickly says *bless you,*
not as a preacher might, or a pious believer,

but like a natural reflex, stimulus/response,

as much a part of the sneeze as what triggered it
or the *thank you* that just as quickly follows,

a rapid exchange unless a multiple seizure

requires a series of blessings and gratitudes.
Maybe it's superstition, a religious hangover

from the centuries when sneezing was thought

to broadcast spirit and leave the soul exposed
to the crafty devil, seeking whom he may devour

even if his only access was through our nostrils.

Maybe it's just manners, a courteous gesture
to one not well from one who, comparatively, is.

Or maybe it's a family habit, one I never learned

from an aunt who cried out *Well! Scat there!*
or a mother who offered a healthy *Gesundheit*

anytime my veteran father was out of the room.

I've seen the famous high-speed photograph
of a kid sneezing a universe from nose and mouth,

bright droplets sprayed at some colossal speed.

A sneeze is no more than irritants and expiration.
But I still like being on the verge of a huge one—

eyes shut, breath held, hands lifted to catch head

as it cannonballs forward after the explosion—
knowing that somebody out there might hear me

and, without thinking, speak that inverse curse,

its terse divine imperative rising like an echo
to the achoo of a fitful sneeze: *bless you.*

Partners

Who's leading, who's following
in this delicate dance between strangers
he's entered into yet again
as in so many stores in so many cities,
each of them carefully looking,
heads cocked, for a certain title that will
suddenly pull them forward,
hands extended, to bring close the book
or recording they've yearned for
for years, or some need just discovered,
claiming their prize without
disturbing the search of this new partner:
he yields to her when quickly
she steps straight ahead to tip one down,
a thoughtful mutual circling
to the left or right, forward or backward
according to each reader's pace
until they reach the end of the shelf or row
and continue, or not, without
ever looking at or brushing into each other
or saying anything except maybe
the quietest "pardon me," touching only
the words or notes they most love,
the sounds that led them to and through
such an intimate routine.

The Tree Man

"Whole lotta baseball bats in there,"
he says, squinting up at the ash.

He straps on spikes then nimbly climbs,
a big kid eager to leave the ground.

A chainsaw dangles from his workbelt—
loud lethal toy to lift and yank.

That powerful finger touches gently:
falling sawdust shimmers in the air.

Ropes follow him wherever he goes,
a puppeteer lowering lassoed limbs.

He hugs the tree like a hungry bear,
a bear whose honey is the tree itself.

Fifty feet up, he stops and studies:
the ash is a problem he must solve,

a case of ever-branching arguments
whose logic flexes underfoot.

He prunes and lops its messy shade:
a schoolkid's drawing, trunk and sticks.

A squall, a downward rush, a thud.
The ropes ascend to his steady hands.

Soon he's the only leaf in the crown.
Soon the old ash is a very tall stump.

Soon it's a thick log laid on the grass,
the tree man walking it, heel to toe.

His every move has been deliberate,
a courtesy to ruthless gravity

and the tree his body gripped for hours,
the phantom ash he still feels pressing

his trunk and legs as if to keep him safe
from all that empty space yawning behind.

"Service Is Our Business"

It used to be black as the insides of a Pennzoil can
whenever we drove this ten-mile stretch of Highway 25
at night from lit-up Asheville back to our gloomy house
in Arden, no stoplights or streetlights anywhere, nothing.

And there's where (during the day) mom would stop for gas,
a Shell filling station in the curve at the foot of a long hill,
a couple of pumps and a little office and a double bay
over which "Service Is Our Business" shone in red plastic

as the smiling proprietor emerged, wiping his large hands,
looking like Glenn Miller on the 78-rpm records she'd play
(I still have them, maiden initials scratched on each label),
like some veteran still wearing his crisp khaki uniform.

He'd bend to the open window and speak to her, then us,
sun polishing his wire rims, starching his cursive name,
brightening the yellow scallop shell stitched to his chest
and the huge one slowly revolving overhead as he began

hooking the nozzle in the tank (gas rushing behind us),
checking (obscured but heard) the oil and radiator water,
cleaning each window (mom laughing loud through hers),
topping off (when needed) the fluids or the air in tires,

then lowering the heavy hood gently, not slamming it down,
and firmly replacing the gas cap behind the license plate,
and taking her offered bills with a thank-you and half-bow
before watching us drive off, shading his eyes as if saluting.

That was 40 years ago. Gas was 28$^{\underline{2}}$. Now that I'm the age
she was then, I wonder: Who *was* that guy? A former boyfriend?
A harmless but steady flirtation? And what was she to him—
another nice housewife to flatter, to keep the business going?

Or were they just a couple of decent lonely people
who enjoyed each other's company for a few public minutes
before returning to work and turning up their tinny radios,
longing to hear "In the Mood" or "Moonlight Serenade" . . . .

That station's long gone. Now it's ten pumps and a mini-mart.
Service *was* his business. And service was her business, too,
a mother serving children every day for over twenty years
until they were old enough to drive their cars away from her.

I pump my own gas then climb into town past strip mall
after strip mall, this local branch of the Dixie Highway
lifting its newly affluent glare into the lost sky every night.
We used to look up at countless stars. Mom loved "Stardust."

I tidy my parents' graves at the cemetery behind K-Mart.
Dusk lurks. That man with the ovaled name might be here
on this hillside with my mother, just one of many customers
queued up in the darkest dark of all, waiting to be served.

Cafeterias

They seemed so glamorous when I was short,
those dim museums of endless comfort food
where we'd line up with other citizens
casting hungry glances into the dining room
and looking ahead toward the black menu board
hung over the stack of still-hot plastic trays
we sometimes had to wipe dry with a napkin
before we could start filing by the dishes
gleaming under prices behind steamy glass
that burned my hand if I touched it for long,
salads and vegetables and meats and breads
and several levels of four-deep desserts.

We could help ourselves at the ends of the line
but had to be served in the middle by people
dressed in crisp white like nurses or orderlies,
wearing hairnets, lifting dripping ladles,
the manager tucking his tie inside his shirt
and trying to keep our slow assembly line
of indecisive eaters shuffling forward,
sliding our trays along the stainless tracks.

I'd squeeze my silverware rolled up in cloth
whenever the fat cashier winked at me,
which was every time my mom and I went out
to our favorite, the S & W
in downtown Asheville, that Art Deco temple
that made me feel like some big-city kid
who could afford to order, without permission,
ground sirloin *au jus*, curly-cut fries,
a doughy roll with two patties of butter,
and the most gigantic wedge of cherry pie
I could reach from the back of the desserts
while trying not to stain my dress-shirt sleeve.

My mom would also let me get a Coke
as long as I'd fetch refills for her coffee
in the thick white cup on the heavy saucer
I sloshed full on the way back to the table
where we mostly ate in satisfied silence
and let all the strangers surrounding us
do the talking, just like in church sometimes
when I'd open my mouth but say nothing

and let the congregation speak for me,
though once I did ask mom if she believed
there might be cafeterias in heaven
where we could eat together now and then
and she laughed, blowing smoke at the ceiling,
and I laughed too, a boy out on the town
eating exactly what I wanted to
and sitting there afterwards with a toothpick
like a man, napkin crumpled on my plate,
my mother smoking, sipping Maxwell House
and sending me back to warm it up again,
we were in no hurry, there would be time

to suck on mints as we walked to the car
and slowly drove the twilit miles back home,
our dishes waited to be cleared and washed
but no sore waitress pressured us to leave,
we just sat at our table like a painting
somebody could study but never buy,
we were that expensive, we were that lucky,
though my mother never said so at the time.

The Tub

Its galvanized surface glistened like frost,
a feathery silver geometry, when dad and I
banged the oval tub into our cramped kitchen
where mom was cooking water on the stove
hot as she could stand it, in four big pots,
then pouring it out in steaming waterfalls,

filling the tub until my sister and I would
step squealing in, gripping the beaded lip
of the metal whose soft roughness scrubbed us
even as dad was trying to scrub off our filth
and mom kept adding clean pots of heat
we avoided like puppies being flea-dipped

but it was no use, we were losing our dirt,
the water was growing soapy-dingy and cool,
it was time to stand up for the final rinse
that sent us shivering into waiting towels
where fresh gooseflesh was rubbed till warm.
How strange that it never seemed strange:

Saturday baths in the kitchen with my sister,
the time dad made bubbles with agitated hands,
the hauling of that tub from some kin's farm
up our basement stairs into the modern light
then—afterwards, slowly, so as not to slosh,
the thin wire handles cutting our soft palms—

out to the back stoop for the loud outpouring
of bathwater gushing into the thirsty dark
before leaning it upside-down against a tree
and drumrolling the corrugated bottom,
leaving it there to dry out and shine all night,
a full-length mirror for the immaculate moon.

Meteor Shower

At first, it's not quite the radiant downpour
predicted or anticipated,

any more than the famous comet
that was only a dull smudge on the sky's page,

but then the meteors start
shooting across the star chart we stare up at,

spoiling those chilly inscrutable mythologies
like scratches on a negative

or little rips in heaven's fabric
that let the light sneak through for a second,

quick thin vapor trails of glory evaporating
almost before we can see them

inside night's enormous brain
whose firing synapses briefly connect the dots

of long-forgotten stories overhead. . . .
Sparse strokes of frost across the blackest pane.

Spitting

Jesus spat on the ground, and made clay of the spittle . . . —John 9:6

I guess it's a guy thing, this ejaculation

of the mouth, this instinctive summoning
of a gob that boys casually meteor

into sand, into dust, into miraculous mud,

marking their own place at the plate,
on the playing field, in the bone-dry world.

Not that every mother doesn't know how

to moisten the corner of her handkerchief
and scrub the hell out of her son's face

before church, slicking down his cowlick

with the leftover. Not that a wronged woman
won't spit in a bastard's leering face.

Not that a tomboy can't handle spittle

for a while, until she probably outgrows it.
But guys never do: it punctuates their speech,

means anger or mirth, says *This is the end*,

clearing a silent space around the speaker
who knows the dramatic value of saliva

(*ptualon* in Greek, hence comic *ptui*).

It's not geezers hawking phlegm into spittoons,
it's not ballplayers befouling Astroturf:

done right, spitting's neat, a delicate matter,

tongue, lips, and air together broadcasting
impeccable opalescent breakdowns of starch.

Precision. Timing. And—ultimately—elevation:

every male has stood at the absolute edge
of a bridge or a skyscraper or a mountaintop

and felt the urge to spit rise up in him

and released a luminous bomb to ride the wind
down to the water or the street or the valley

where he just was, like some cartoon saint

lounging on a cloud (the expectoration of angels)
who every now and then leans over the edge

to take aim on the world that he once walked

and darken it again with the damp little stain
his spit will leave if it ever hits the ground.

Rosin Bag

A sticky little cloud
I'd toss into the air
behind the pitcher's mound,
bouncing it off the back
of my ungloved right hand
with a puff of pale dust,
catching and squeezing it
until sweet tackiness
covered my sweaty palm
and I could grip the ball
so flawlessly no bat
had the remotest chance,
I lift it to my face
again in this dugout
and smell the gummy pines
behind my parents' house
I'd climb until the sap
had smeared its adhesive
on all my skin and clothes,
those sold trees now cut down
and converted to boards
for fancy pine boxes
above and under ground
or maybe pulverized
until they're nothing more
than an ounce of powder
inside a sewn cloth sack,
this evergreen sachet
whose incense will outlast
my flesh and nicest suit
when it's buried with me.

Spigot with Imaginary Animals

—German, city of Augsburg, c. 1550-1560

Whatever prince commissioned this fancy faucet
was sick of Luther and Melanchthon and austere Calvin,
the relentless pressure of salvation-by-faith-not-works,

just as he'd long ago wearied of the local Catholics,
so corrupt, so expensive, so insufferably smug.

He ordered this pagan tap fashioned from bronze,
a couple of wide-eyed grotesque refugees escaped
from a manuscript's margin or cathedral's lofty gutter:

a fish-like handle whose tail, curled up behind its head,
was turned to release liquid into the outstretched throat

of the gargoyle spout whose enormous upper lip,
flared far back in joyful anger or angry joy,
allowed for the rapid filling of bowls and tankards

and, quite late at night, the mouth of a thirsty prince
who saw in this living spigot his own metamorphosis

into something no longer human, a bottomless gullet
gloriously sheathed with leafy scales or scaly leaves
overlapping on a creature just beginning to bud,

utterly inarticulate and happy, untroubled by God,
transformed by wine that was nothing more than wine.

The Lessons

You could see it, or it could see you, anywhere in town,
the county jail crowning the lofty granite courthouse.
I watched it as I rode into Asheville for weekly church;

it watched me as I sat in First Baptist's Sunday School
a couple of blocks away, supposedly learning the lessons
that would save me from ending up in a place like that.

One year Mr. Creech was our teacher, a retired lawyer
so nearsighted and hard of hearing he seemed oblivious
to our brilliant adolescent jokes and caricatures.

But one day he stood up and started class by announcing,
"Boys, we're going over to the jail to teach Sunday School,"
and led our astonished gang out of the education wing

across to the courthouse and onto a cramped elevator
whose uniformed black operator never once looked at us,
yanking the heavy doors shut, punching the last number,

lifting our cell through a dozen floors emptied of people,
jerking us to a stop. "Penthouse!" he cried, and suddenly
we were in jail, being frisked and questioned, surrounded

by guns and keys and heavy metal gates locked behind us.
Mr. Creech was mild as ever, there in the narrow cellblock.
"Good morning, gentlemen," he said, and smiled, and began

teaching about Paul and Silas locked in a dismal prison,
leaving us boys to note the caged lights and grimy iron grids,
the breathtaking stench of toilets, vomit, and body odor,

the restless shadowy movements of criminals in their cells,
squeaking on bunks, shuffling shoes, squeezing bars thick as wrists
with hands that looked almost dead in such lousy wattage:

these were the lessons that old man wanted to teach us.
"And at midnight, they prayed and sang praises unto the Lord,"
he read. "We all know what singing is; but what is prayer?

Son?" he turned and asked, pulling me steadily forward,
"can you tell us what it is?" I thought I would gag or faint
if I opened my mouth, so I just stood there mute. "Oh *son,*"

came a deep sarcastic echo, "can you tell us what it is?"
"Come over here and tell me what *this* is," a man whispered,
and the Amens that followed unlocked something in me:

"Prayer," I said, lifting my eyes to the low stained ceiling,
"prayer is just talking with God, that's all." Mr. Creech paused,
pinching my shoulder hard before he said, "just talking *to* God,"

then concluded our lesson with a prayer and altar call
though the prisoners never bowed their heads or responded:
they kept staring at me as I tried to hide behind my friends,

reaching for but not quite touching us as we left the jail,
boys who might never be any farther away from God
than high in that hellish heaven above that mountain town.

"Helen, Come Forth!"

We didn't know or care that it all started
with a kitchen fire up at Zealandia,
the hilltop mansion built by Colonel Brown
when he came back to Asheville a rich man
from decades of New Zealand sheep farming,
a flash fire in which a servingwoman
named Helen lost her infant girl Ellen,
left to sleep in a basket by the stove:
men had to hold her back from rushing in
and dying with her daughter in the blaze,

but she jerked free and ran the other way
so they let her go into the mountain night,
wild with grief, screaming her baby's name.
They found her later, dangling from an oak.
She hanged herself with her own apron strings.
And so began the legend of her ghost,
a troubled vapor wandering the grounds
for several restless months, sobbing, "Ellen!",
her voice a mournful stirring of cold wind
just this side of the threshold of hearing.

And then she went away, until, years later,
a moonshine couple said that she appeared
after they held hands and called out, "Helen!",
gliding toward them one Halloween midnight
across the frosty lawn at Zealandia,
her flowing gown aflame, her pale arms wide.
They barely got their car to start in time
but came back next October thirty-first,
ready to conjure Helen and be thrilled,
clinging to each other in the haunted dark.

That story spread all over the mountains.
Our local version of the Helen tale
as we all heard it in south Buncombe County
after half a century of changes
was that she died on nearby Mount Royal
in a housefire set by her jealous husband,
standing on the second-floor balcony
so he could watch her body feed the flames,
the last tongues to taste her blazing beauty.
"Helen, come forth!" he'd cried, and so did we,

not just on Halloween but anytime
we parked up there and felt melodramatic,
delivering the line into the sky
and waiting for an echo from the valley,
or a laugh from one of the cars behind us,
or maybe—if the moon and clouds were right—
a helpless shivery shortness of breath
as something almost took shape just ahead,
a trick of light and air and the late hour
moving toward something in us that almost believed.

Roof Ball

The roof was an uphill grade I'd bomb for hours
with any rubber ball that had some bounce,
tossing it high and far away enough
that I'd have to haul ass to haul it in,
Mantle making the Series-clinching out.

I pitched, I caught, I played my yard's flat field.
How close could I come to the shingled peak
without losing the ball to the backyard side,
a homer that just cleared the lofty fence?
Those were the hardest drives to time and stop.

How close could I come to the sludgy gutter
without clipping it or getting the ball stuck?
Those were the most melodramatic catches,
crashing into the bushes or the house
at top speed, arms outstretched, to save the day.

I only played when the family was gone.
Mom would have warned me not to hurt myself
or chip the shingles or loosen the gutters.
Dad would have told me he was trying to sleep
or come outside and tried to play with me

but I liked this lonely game that I controlled,
the heave, the thump, the run, the graceful snatch
a sort of prayer my body said for years,
my open face and hands upraised to heaven,
filling that haunted attic with dumb noise.

Curtains

The heavy velvet curtains, thick as sleep,
seal off the stage and its imminent music.

The players gather in noon; we wait in dusk.
A line of light hums under the pleated hem.

Decades of dust and notes and long applause
weigh down the massive cataract of fabric.

Two steady hands can make this hung wall part,
then slam the swaying halves softly together.

Suddenly it ripples, as if alive,
like something under its skin wants to get out.

What or who is stuck on that other side?
Are they trying to escape, or let us in?

It's just a poking elbow, hip, or hand—
my son's conductor, searching for the seam.

My son's extremities, weeks before birth.
My father's skeleton, haunting dying flesh.

The curtains open on rows of ready bodies.
They close on rooms filled with music already gone.

Whistling

You just put your lips together and blow. —Lauren Bacall

"In heaven," my Jesuit professor would say,

"the angels may perform Bach in concert
but in private they always whistle Mozart!"

And then he'd pucker up and kiss the air

in that stale classroom until it quivered
with celestial melodies so lucid and profound

the texts were singing when we turned to them.

That's the miracle, how whistling converts
mere breathing into music, prose into poetry,

the foulest mouth into the sweetest instrument:

even the bitter old poet whose acid tongue
disfigured every doomed student in his class

warbled gentle solos while strolling campus,

even my father—whom I never heard sing—sang
by blowing a perpetual medley of '40s tunes,

a swinging soundtrack to our dull home movie.

It can be functional, a piercing signal
involving teeth on lips or fingers in mouth

to call back far-off kids or dogs or taxis,

or a wolfish appreciation of passing beauty,
or a genuine glissando of astonishment;

it could be learned, perhaps, from a tutor

expert in contracting lips to a perfect circle
and making breath resonate in the mouth-cavity

without any vibration of the vocal cords;

but it's best when spontaneous, self-taught,
a rhythmic hissing whisper practiced alone

until one day you break through to a tone,

a note, a phrase, a tune, an actual song
somebody else might be able to recognize,

you'll never exhale in quite the same way again,

at any moment your body might just blossom
into a forgotten melody, or an improvised one,

filling the shower or stairwell or open air

with gloriously imperfect whistling that will
beget other whistling worlds without end.

Icewater in a Tumbler

All the dying man asked for
was icewater in a tumbler on his bedside table

so he could reach and touch it
and make that cold glass fog up one last time,

condensation obscuring
his view of the dim sickroom through that lens

for a few sweating minutes
until his fingers had lost their heat to the water

and the melted ice had poured
its current deep into his strangely distant body

and the parched air had begun
sipping the tumbler until empty, the eyes until dry.

Old Pillow

Uncased, it's a bulging ceiling
stained by seepage from a leaky roof.

How could her sleeping head have sweated so,
its yellow dreams sinking
through pillowcases for years, whatever the season,
soaking this ticking?

It's a swollen sheet of paper
troubled by a nightmare wash of clouds.

What smoky signals was her brain sending
to the pillow's foam brain
as she lay beside him through the cool still nights,
quietly oozing away?

It's a spirit-headstone, faintly marbled.
It's the veronica that some god leaves through us.

Shinemaster

I don't know why the fabulous griffin—lifting
its huge eagle beak and wings, its long lion tail
and clearly unshod right front paw—ever became
part of the name and logo of this shoeshine kit

but there it is, in golden profile on the label:
Griffin Shinemaster, a squat honey-oak casket
my father would bring from his bedroom closet
on those rare dress-up occasions that required

his shoes to look as sharp as his suit and hat,
a heavy style all creases and cuffs and edges.
He'd let me unlace his wingtips, their perforation
a swirling code my fingertips couldn't crack,

then he'd snap open the brass lock, lift the lid,
and spread his tools across an unfolded *Times*:
the worn-out undershirt for prefatory cleaning;
the little brush for daubing polish from the tin

and scrubbing it gently into the scuffed uppers,
the toe, the vamp, the dented tongue, the heel;
the old toothbrush for carefully blacking the soles;
the big flat brush for converting that dull primer

into a shine, a sheen, one polish-flecked hand
inside the shoe turning it while the other buffed;
and finally, half of mom's maroon woolen scarf
for reviving, with slick friction, the lapsed dazzle

from each shoe as he slipped it on and fitted
its slick leather sole onto the wooden footprint
screwed to the kit's lid at a thirty-degree angle,
blurred hands and cloth converting the Florsheims

to greater-than-original glory, a transfigured state.
The last time he used this kit was for mom's funeral.
The last time he wore those wingtips was at his own.
The first time I opened the Shinemaster afterwards,

that new-shoe smell was all his, piercing as cedar.
I don't know why the flightless hunched-over kiwi
ever came to be the mascot of a brand of polish,
but I do know how to take this leftover cordovan

and make a pair of tired dress shoes really gleam,
my feet flashing in the sun as they stride between
the quick and the dead, winged heel to wingtip,
my father's shining step still mastering the air.

Surely

As we stood shivering at the pasture's crest,
watching last light cling like dew to the grass,

suddenly they were straight overhead, the geese
making their dusk migration to an upvalley pond

though without their usual lofty honking racket:
they were flying in absolute silence and so low

we could hear the machinery of their wings working—
not a feathery whoosh but a hard steady whirring

like dozens of bicycle chains being downshifted
as the racers start sprinting to the dark finish line,

the geese relentlessly pulling away toward victory
behind the ridge already blacker than night sky

as you will surely leave me someday, and I you,
standing in strange fields, forsaken yet lifted up.

author photo by Philip McFee